Moving in Harmony

An Updated Polity for The United Methodist Church in Africa

by

Rev. Nday Bondo

Africa Ministry Series

Moving in Harmony

An Updated Polity for The United Methodist Church in Africa

Cover and interior design: Karin Wizer
Cover photo: Lanecia Rouse
Typesetting: PerfecType, Nashville, TN

ISBN 978-0-88177-868-7

Contents

Introduction

Church polity has to do with the form of governance, organization, administration, legislation, rule, and structures used by the church to govern itself. The United Methodist Church (UMC) polity is found in *The Book of Discipline of the United Methodist Church*. This book of law and discipline of the UMC is published and updated every four years following the General Conference meeting. *The Book of Discipline* contains all the necessary information for governance of the UMC polity.

The UMC, being a connectional church, uses the same *Book of Discipline* and polity all over the world with some adjustments and adaptations made by regional conferences outside the United States, or central conferences, as allowed since the 1920 General Conference.

> A central conference shall have power to make such changes and adaptations of the *Book of Discipline* as the special conditions and the mission of the church in the area require, especially concerning the organization and administration of the work on local church, district, and annual conference levels, provided that no action shall be taken that is contrary to the Constitution and the General Rules of The United Methodist Church, and provided that the spirit of connectional relationship is kept between the local and the general church. (¶ 543.7)

Since its inception, the Africa Central Conference has published four central conference editions of *The Book of Discipline*. The first was published in 1943, the second in 1948, the third in 1956, and the latest edition in 1990. In 1992, a new central conference, the Congo Central Conference, was created within the Africa Central Conference. Both central conferences have been using the same edition of *The Book of Discipline* for twenty years without publishing a new edition.

Considering that UMC polity undergoes changes every four years at General Conference, an updated *Book of Discipline* for the Africa Central Conferences is long overdue.

The Church in Africa is ill-informed about UMC polity due to lack of access to updated information from the most recent *Book of Discipline.* Many churches in Africa are still using outdated polity. Unbelievably, some people still refer to *The Book of Discipline of the Methodist Church* 1956, while others are struggling to implement the polity from the 1990 *Book of Discipline, Africa Central Conference edition*. As a whole, the Church in Africa is many years behind the current accepted United Methodist polity.

Therefore, this project hopes to bring the most relevant and up-to-date information from *The Book of Discipline* 2008 to the African Methodist Church, in order that it can join and move in harmony with the polity of the general church.

This work is not meant to be the Africa Central Conference Book of Discipline of the UMC. The author lacks the power and authority to create such a resource. Instead, this work is an effort to highlight the major changes that have occurred over years to the UMC polity, using primarily the 2008 and 2004 editions of the *Book of Discipline* to show changes in comparison with previous editions. *The United Methodist Handbook*, published in 2009, has also served as a source for summarized information on general agencies. Chapters in this book are organized following the order of the *Book of Discipline.*

The first chapter deals with the local church. A lot of changes have been made at this level, but implementation is problematic. There is some resistance to change from the clergy, given the fact that changes are empowering laity in the church. Many pastors opt for the status quo, instead of following polity changes. Laity as well are hesitant to see themselves as part of the ministry of all believers because they are accustomed to clergy doing everything.

Chapter 2 deals with the ministry of the ordained, or the clergy. There are a lot of discrepancies in the organization of clergy in Africa in light of major changes at the 1996 General Conference. Here again, churches in Africa will be asked to work together to implement these changes in order to preserve the Methodist connectionalism.

The third chapter concentrates on superintendency, dealing with special ministry of the ordained achieved by bishops and district superintendents. Emphasis is placed on the appointment-making process performed by the superintendency. The process needs to be done with care, respecting procedures in order to maintain itinerancy in the UMC.

In Chapter 4 we discuss the organization of conferences. At this level structures are similar, with some resistance noted, especially at the annual conference and district conference levels. One cannot attribute the lack of implementation of these changes to ignorance, given that all annual conferences are represented at General and central conference sessions.

The fifth chapter describes the UMC agencies, about which little is known in Africa. Many people only have knowledge of the General Board of Global Ministries (GBGM) because of the presence of missionaries in Africa. This ignorance is due to a lack of emphasis on these important structures put into place by the general church to achieve its mission. This chapter will give general information about these agencies so that the church in Africa may take advantage of these agencies in order to develop more fully as central conferences. Elaborate details are found in the 2008 *Book of Discipline*.

Chapter 6, the shortest, deals with the UMC system of governance. Few changes occurred to the system. A conclusion and some recommendations close this book.

Information found in this book is accurate but not complete. There may be some aspects of UMC polity that are not mentioned. Pastors and lay leaders are strongly encouraged to have their own copies of *The Book of Discipline* to familiarize themselves with changes.

Chapter 1

The Local Church

The local church is a connectional society of persons who have been baptized, have professed their faith in Christ, and have assumed the vows of membership in The United Methodist Church. *They gather in fellowship to hear the* Word *of* God, *receive the sacraments, praise and worship the triune God, and carry forward the work that* Christ *has committed to his church. Such a society of believers, being within* The United Methodist Church *[is] subject to its* Discipline. . . .

—*The Book of Discipline of* The United Methodist Church 2008 (¶ 203)

The local church does not work in isolation, with its own structure, organization, and administration. Throughout the UMC, the local church follows a common organization and administration enabling anyone moving in the church connection to minister and to be ministered to according to the United Methodist tradition. In a local UMC, leaders and congregations are connected, accountable to one another, and empowered to be in ministry around the world.

Church Membership

Membership in the UMC includes all believers without regard to race, color, national origin, disability, or economic conditions. A United Methodist member in the local church belongs to the worldwide United Methodist connection and the universal church (holy catholic church, as proclaimed in the creeds). (*The Book of Discipline of The United Methodist Church* 2008, ¶ 4)

> ¶ 215 *Definition of Membership*—The membership of a local United Methodist Church shall include all people who have been baptized and all people who have professed their faith.
>
> 1. The baptized membership of a local United Methodist church shall include all baptized people who have received Christian baptism in the local congregation or elsewhere, or whose membership has been transferred to the local United Methodist church subsequent to baptism in some other congregation.
> 2. The professing membership of a local United Methodist church shall include all baptized people who have come into membership by profession of faith through appropriate services of the baptismal covenant in the ritual or by transfer from other churches.
> 3. For statistical purposes, church membership is equated to the number of people listed on the roll of professing members.

The Book of Discipline 1980 ¶ 209 expresses the same definition of membership in the following words: "The membership of a local United Methodist Church shall include all baptized persons who have come into membership by confession of faith or transfer."

There is a category of membership preparing believers for full or professing membership called preparatory membership. It comprises:

- Those who are not yet baptized but wishing to be members of the UMC
- Baptized infants

- People coming from other Christian denominations and joining the UMC
- United Methodist members who are under church discipline

Preparatory members undergo training during a reasonable time prior to their confirmation and reception as professing members.

The Book of Discipline Africa Central Conference Edition 1990 in ¶ 112 uses the terms *catechumens, probationary members,* and *full members* in categorizing church membership. Catechumens and probationary members can fit in the category of preparatory members while full members are those called *professing members* in *The Book of Discipline* 2008.

Confirmation of baptized infants is practiced on children aged twelve years and older. However, a child who is younger than twelve years can be confirmed at the pastor's discretion if the child personally wishes it. Professing membership also includes members from chaplaincies supervised by United Methodist chaplains.

Organization and Administration

The church in Africa lacks updated information concerning the organization and administration of the local church. It is at this level that a lot has to be said and done to improve UMC polity in Africa. These improvements are elaborated in detail below from *The Book of Discipline* 2008:

> The local church shall be organized so that it can pursue its primary task and mission in the context of its own community—reaching out and receiving with joy all who will respond; encouraging people in their relationship with God and inviting them to commitment to God's love in Jesus Christ; providing opportunities for them to seek strengthening and growth in spiritual formation; and

> supporting them to live lovingly and justly in the power of the Holy Spirit as faithful disciples.
>
> In carrying out its primary task, it shall be organized so that adequate provision is made for these basic responsibilities: (1) planning and implementing a program of nurture, outreach, and witness for persons and families within and without the congregation; (2) providing for effective pastoral and lay leadership; (3) providing for financial support, physical facilities, and the legal obligations of the church; (4) utilizing the appropriate relationships and resources of the district and annual conference; . . . (¶ 243)

In order to achieve the above tasks and responsibilities,

> The basic organizational plan for the local church shall include provision for the following units: a charge conference, a church council, a committee on pastor-parish relations, a board of trustees, a committee on finance, a committee on nominations and leadership development, and such other elected leaders, commissions, councils, committees, and task forces as the charge conference may determine. . . . (¶ 244)

The Charge Conference

The charge conference is the basic unit in the connectional system of the UMC within the pastoral charge. It is the connecting link between the local church and the general church. It has the general oversight of the church council.

- ". . . It shall meet annually . . . It may meet at other times" as special sessions "called by the district superintendent after consultation with the pastor of the charge, or by the pastor with the written consent of the district superintendent." (¶¶ 246.1. and 7.)

- "The membership of the charge conference shall be all members of the church council . . . , together with retired ordained ministers and retired diaconal ministers who elect to hold their membership in said charge conference. . . . (¶ 246.2)
- "The district superintendent shall fix the time of meetings of the charge conference" while "the charge conference determines the place of meeting." (¶ 246.4)
- "The district superintendent shall preside at the meetings of the charge conference or may designate an elder to preside." (¶ 246.5)
- "A **joint charge conference** for two or more pastoral charges may be held at the same time and place, as the district superintendent may determine." (¶ 246.10)
- "The charge conference, the district superintendent, and the pastor shall organize and administer the pastoral charge and churches according to the policies and plans herein set forth." (¶ 247.2)
- "The primary responsibilities of the charge conference . . . shall be to review and evaluate the total mission and ministry of the church . . . , receive reports, and adopt objectives and goals recommended by the church council that are in keeping with the objectives of the United Methodist Church." (¶ 247.3)

The UMC at the local church level, before the institution of the charge conference, was governed by the quarterly conference. African Methodism in some areas continued to use such a structure up to the 1990s. Some other churches have applied the structure of charge conferences but have misunderstood or misused it. Oftentimes the charge conference is held as a quarterly conference, instead of annually per *The*

Discipline. Lack of access to updated information is one of the factors contributing to this situation.

A charge conference and/or a joint charge conference chaired by the district superintendent (DS) reflect connectionalism in the UMC. A local church is not autonomous and independent. It shares with others for success in ministry. A charge conference may be convened as the church conference, extending the vote to all professing members of the local church present at such meetings. The purpose of invoking a church conference is to encourage broader participation by members of the church.

A charge conference may be called at the discretion of the DS or following a request by the pastor, the church council, or ten percent of the professing membership.

The Church Council

The church council is the administrative, or executive, agency of the charge conference.

> The church council shall provide for planning and implementing a program of nurture, outreach, witness, and resources in the local church. It shall also provide for the administration of its organization and temporal life. . . . (¶ 252.1)

In brief, the church council is the administrative and programmatic body of the church.

- "The council shall meet at least quarterly. The chairperson or the pastor may call special meetings." (¶ 252.3.a.)
- ". . . It is recommended that the first agenda item at each meeting be related to [the local church's] ministries of nurture, outreach, and witness." In addition the agenda should include attention to

administrative and support responsibilities, review of membership, and filling vacancies occurring among the lay officers of the church. (¶¶ 252.3.b. and 4)

- ". . . The membership of the [church] council . . . shall include but not be limited to: *a*) the chairperson of the church council; *b*) the lay leader; *c*) the chairperson and/or a representative of the pastor-parish relations committee; *d*) the chairperson and/or a representative of the committee on finance; *e*) the chairperson and/or a representative of the board of trustees; *f*) the church treasurer; *g*) a lay member to annual conference; *h*) the president and/or a representative of the United Methodist Men; *i*) the president and/or a representative of the United Methodist Women; *j*) a young adult representative; *k*) a representative of the United Methodist Youth; [and] *l*) the pastor(s)." (¶ 252.5)

The structure of the *church council* as described in *The Book of Discipline* 2008 has undergone many changes in the history of UMC polity. *The Book of Doctrines and Discipline of the Methodist Church* 1956 in ¶¶ 206–296 presents the official board as the structure similar to the church council. The differences reside in the frequency of meetings and the chairpersons. The official board was meeting monthly, chaired by the pastor, whereas the church council is a quarterly meeting chaired by laypersons. The church council empowers laypeople and fully involves them in church leadership. The administrative council is mentioned in *The Book of Discipline* 1980 as a combination of the administrative board and the council on ministries (¶ 245.1.a).

After the official board, the administrative board became the executive structure of the UMC. *The Book of Discipline* 1980 (¶ 254.1) names the following responsibilities to the administration board for administering the organization of the local church: the council on ministries, the committee on nominations and personnel, the committee on pastor-parish relations, the committee on finance and the trustees.

The Book of Discipline 1988 (¶ 252.1) describes the administrative council as both the administrative body and the programmatic body. This new development is not alluded to in *The Book of Discipline* 1990, *Africa Central Conference Edition* that maintains the administrative board structure including its five components as already mentioned above. The term *church council* appears in *The Book of Discipline* 1996 (¶ 254). This term appears as the new appellation replacing the administrative board. From there, the term *council on ministries* disappears and a new term, *specialized ministries*, appears to cover the council on ministries' responsibilities.

The Council on Ministries

This is the programmatic body of the church council, though the term itself has disappeared from *The Book of Discipline* as of 1996 and has been replaced by the term *specialized ministries*. *Council on ministries* is still the term used in Africa. In some episcopal areas, this term is replaced by *connectional ministries*, which will be described in the chapter dealing with conferences.

Specialized ministries from *The Book of Discipline* 2008 (¶¶ 253–257) may elect annually coordinators in the following areas:

- "Age-Level, Family and Specialized-Ministries": children's ministries, youth ministries, adult ministries, and family ministries
- Other ministries may include: "education, evangelism, higher education and campus ministry, missions, . . . stewardship, worship," etc.

Specialized ministries include the following program ministries:

- Church School and Small-Group Ministries for supporting the formation of Christian disciples focused on the transformation of the world. These may include,

- Children's ministries
- Young people's ministries
- Civic youth-serving agencies and scouting ministries
- United Methodist Women
- United Methodist Men

The specialized ministries are the same as the ministries found under the council on ministries in *The Africa Central Conference Book of Discipline* 1990. And the ministries of the council are arranged into three categories:

- The small groups ministries: class meetings, Sunday schools, Bible study groups.
- Work areas: evangelism and membership, worship and music, Christian social concerns, stewardship, education, women's work, etc.
- Program agencies: they represent the program ministries found in *The Book of Discipline* 2008.

Therefore, the use of the term *council on ministries* is valid and useful in the context of the UMC in Africa. The council on ministries is the programmatic body of the church council. The term is still in use in Africa. It is supported by ¶ 252.5 of *The Book of Discipline* 2008, referring to the church council membership in these words, "The membership shall include but not be limited to the following . . ." The phrase *but not limited* might have been used in Africa to consider the council on ministries as part of the church council.

The council on ministries shall consider, develop, and coordinate goals and program proposals for the church's mission. It shall receive and, where possible, utilize resources for missions provided by the district, annual, central, and general councils on ministries or connectional ministries, boards and agencies, and shall coordinate these resources with the church's plan for ministries. In connection with what has been said, the council on ministries is connected to the same offices found at district, annual, central, and general conference levels.

The council on ministries shall meet at least quarterly before the church council's meeting. Its membership includes:

- The council on ministries chairperson
- The chairperson of the church council
- The lay leader
- The pastor(s)
- The work area chairs: evangelism, Christian education, stewardship, worship
- The small group chairs: class leaders, Sunday school leader
- The program ministries: United Methodist Men, United Methodist Women, and United Methodist Youth Fellowship (see ¶¶ 253–257)

The chairperson of the council on ministries shall be a layperson or a minister who is not a member of the local church staff. The council on ministries works in connection with the administrative committees of the church council, namely the committee on finance, to request the financial resources needed to undergird the ministries it has developed; the pastor-parish relations committee regarding the professional and other staff positions needed to carry out the program projected by the council; and the committee on lay leadership development in nominating candidates for ministries chairs.

The council on ministries is amenable to the church council to which it shall submit its goals and program plans for revision and appropriate action. Upon adoption of the goals and program plans by the church council, the council on ministries shall implement and evaluate the goals and program plans that are assigned.

There is no equivalent structure to the council on ministries in the 1956 *Discipline*. It may be compared to the lay leadership position, given that all ministries are chaired by laypeople. The creation of the council on ministries caused a job conflict between the local church lay leader and the council on ministries chairperson.

According to the 1956 *Doctrines and Discipline of the Methodist Church* ¶ 288, the church lay leader is responsible for the presentation of the program to the board for the adoption of plans necessary to carry out the work, and for continued leadership to make it effective. The lay leader shall make a report to each regular session of the board, and to the quarterly conference. Those statements make it clear that the council on ministries has now taken on these church leadership responsibilities. So what role does the church lay leader play in the new structure?

All the Books of Discipline using the new structure give the following responsibilities to the church lay leader (¶ 251):

- "Fostering awareness of the role of laity both within the congregation" and through the outreach and witness ministries.
- Serving as "an interpreter of the actions and programs of the annual conference and the general Church." For the lay leader to be well "equipped to comply with this responsibility, it is recommended that a lay leader also serve as a lay member of annual conference," and ex officio member of the charge conference, councils and administrative committees of the local church.
- "Assisting in advising the church council of opportunities available and the needs expressed for a more effective ministry of the church through its laity in the community."

Committee on Lay Leadership Development

This is an administrative committee in the local church whose charge is "to identify, develop, deploy, evaluate, and monitor Christian spiritual leadership for the local congregation" (¶ 258.1). The committee recommends "to the charge conference, at its annual session, the names of people to serve as officers and leaders of designated ministries of the church council" as follows (see ¶ 249):

- Chairperson of the church council
- The council on ministries chairperson, or the chairperson of connectional ministries
- The committee on lay leadership
- The committee on pastor-parish relations and its chairperson
- The chairperson and additional members of the committee on finance; the financial secretary, and the church treasurer
- The board of trustees (see ¶ 2532)
- The lay leader(s)
- The lay member(s) of the annual conference
- The recording secretary
- The work area chairs: evangelism, Christian education, stewardship, worship (see ¶ 254)
- The small groups chairs: class leaders, Sunday school leader (see ¶ 255)
- The coordinator of youth ministries (see ¶ 253)

The program ministries leaders of the United Methodist Men, United Methodist Women, and United Methodist Youth Fellowship are elected by their respective organizations (see ¶ 256.5.5, for example) and work under the church council.

Although the committee recommends people be elected, the floor has the right to add members during the election process.

This committee is to be composed of not more than nine persons, in addition to the pastor and the lay leader. The pastor shall be the chairperson and a layperson elected by the committee shall serve as the vice chairperson of the committee. (¶ 258.1.c.)

Where vacancies occur during the year, nominees shall be elected by the church council with the permission of the DS. The committee on lay leadership development shall serve throughout the year to guide the church council on matters regarding the leadership of the congregation. It does not deal with matters pertaining to employed staff. (¶ 258.1.d.)

The Discipline of the Methodist Church in Africa 1944 used the name *committee on nominations* with the particularity that it gave power to the pastor to recommend leaders for election to the quarterly conference on behalf of the committee (¶ 346.1). The same committee maintained the same name in the 1956 *Disciplines and Doctrines of the Methodist Church* (¶ 145.1). The committee on lay leadership development was previously called *committee on nominations and personnel*. The Books of Discipline from 1996 onward are using the appellation "committee on leadership development," removing the term *personnel* from the committee because current committee structure no longer deals with the recruitment of employed staff or personnel.

At this point, one can understand the role played by the pastor of the Methodist Church in Africa and why some of the pastors still feel empowered to nominate and assign people to some positions without following required procedures.

Committee on Pastor-Parish Relations or Staff-Parish Relations

This is a committee working as a connector between the pastor and/or the staff and the parish or congregation. It is "composed of not fewer than five nor more than nine persons. . . . In addition, the lay leader, . . . a lay member of the annual conference" and the pastor are to be members. "No staff member or immediate family member of a pastor or staff member may serve on the committee. Only one person from an immediate family residing in the same household shall serve on the committee." Restrictions on the membership of the committee may have been given as provisions to keep objectivity and impartiality of the committee when it comes to vote on matters pertaining to staff members. (¶ 258.2.a.). The committee is to meet at least quarterly (¶ 258.2.e.).

The roles of the pastor-parish relations committee include, but are not limited to (¶ 258.2.g.):

On behalf of the pastor:

- "To encourage, strengthen, nurture, support, and respect the pastor(s) and staff and their family(s)."
- "To confer with and counsel the pastor(s) and staff on the matters pertaining to the effectiveness of ministry [and] relationships with the congregation."
- "To provide evaluation at least annually for the use of the pastor(s) and staff in an ongoing effective ministry. . . ."
- To cooperate with the district superintendent and the bishop in an advisory capacity.

On behalf of the parish, the committee communicates and interprets to the congregation the nature and function of ministry in the UMC regarding open itinerancy, the preparation for ordained ministry, and the ministerial education fund.

Working as a personnel committee:

- "To develop and approve written job descriptions and titles for associate pastors and other staff members . . . "
- "To recommend to the church council . . . the professional and other staff positions . . . needed to carry out the work of the church or charge."
- "To enlist, interview, evaluate, review, and recommend annually to the charge conference lay preachers and persons for candidacy for ordained ministry. . . ."

It is amazing that this committee was already mentioned in the 1956 *Disciplines and Doctrines of the Methodist Church* under the name "committee on pastoral relations." However, this committee seems not to have been as effective and organized as it is today in Africa. Lay leaders were playing the role of the committee on pastoral relations in a limited manner. They were bringing parish concerns to the pastor(s) but they were dealing more with the parish ministerial support from the congregation to their pastor. They were not expected to evaluate their pastors and be consulted by the district superintendent or the bishop concerning their pastors. The pastors' annual conference membership has often been used to prevent lay people from dealing with pastors' assessments. In addition, few local churches in Africa have paid staff members. Lay people fill some positions and they work for free. Therefore, Africa talks more of the committee on pastor-parish relations than staff-parish relations.

Board of Trustees

"The board of trustees shall have the supervision, oversight, and care of all real property owned by the local church and of all property and equipment acquired directly by the local church or by any society, board, class, commission, or similar organization connected therewith. . . . [It] shall review annually the adequacy of these properties, liability, and crime insurance coverage on church-owned property, buildings, and equipment" to make sure church property is "properly protected against risks" (¶¶ 2532.1. and 2).

The board of trustees is one of the local church structures that has maintained its organization for many quadrennia. It consists of not fewer than three, but no more than nine persons elected by the charge or church conference, to serve for a term of three years. It elects from its membership a chairperson, a vice chairperson, a secretary, and if needed, a treasurer to hold office for a term of one year.

The board of trustees at the local church level deals with the supervision and care of church property, especially securing and protecting church property against unjustifiable loss.

Committee on Finance

> All financial askings to be included in the annual budget of the local church shall be submitted to the committee on finance. The committee on finance shall compile

> annually a complete budget for the local church and submit it to the church council for review and adoption. The committee on finance shall be charged with responsibility for developing and implementing plans that will raise sufficient income to meet the budget adopted by the church council. (¶ 258.4)

The Committee on Finance is "composed of the chairperson; the pastor(s); a lay member of the annual conference; the chairperson of the church council; the chairperson or representative of the committee on pastor-parish relations; a representative of the trustees to be selected by the trustees; the chairperson of the ministry group on stewardship; the lay leader; the financial secretary; the treasurer; the church business administrator; and other members to be added as the charge conference may determine" (¶ 258.4).

In many annual conferences in Africa, positions of the ministry group on stewardship and the church business administrator are not yet organized, and therefore are often overlooked as members of the committee on finance.

Many previous books of discipline maintain the same structure. *The Discipline of the Methodist Church in Africa* 1944 talked of the finance committee that was preparing the local budget in collaboration with the pastor and the treasurer (¶ 373). *The Discipline of the Methodist Church* 1956 called it a commission on stewardship and finance. It played the same role as in the current structure. This makes it sound as if the treasurer was not part of the finance committee and he/she was not amenable to the committee. In ¶ 357, the treasurer was elected annually by the quarterly conference on nomination of the pastor or on nomination of a committee of which the pastor should be chairperson. From this statement, the appointment of a treasurer seems to have been made at the pastor's discretion. This procedure has been applied up to now by some churches despite the change in the structure that relieves pastors from the misconception that they were choosing treasurers who could manipulate the finances for their interests.

Ex Officio Membership

The church has a category of members called *ex officio members*. An ex officio member is a member of a body (a board, committee, council) and is part of the body by virtue of holding another office. For example, if the committee on finance constitutes a commission consisting of a treasurer and three other members appointed for a purpose, the treasurer is said to be ex officio member of the finance commission since he or she is automatically a member of that commission by virtue of the fact that he or she holds the office of treasurer.

Describing the administrative board of the local church, *The Book of Discipline* 1992 in its ¶ 255 states, "The pastor shall be the administrative officer, and as such shall be an ex officio member of all conferences, boards, councils, commissions, committees, and task forces, unless restricted by the Discipline." In the UMC, the pastor and the lay leader are ex officio members of boards, committees, and councils, by virtue of their positions in the local church. The chairs of committees and councils are found to be members of other committees and councils because of the positions they hold.

Ex officio members are afforded the same rights as other members, including debate and making formal motions. However, there are some restrictions regarding voting. For instance, pastors are ex officio members of the committee on finance. They are restricted from voting because the committee deals with the financial support of pastors, and if the latter are allowed to vote, they may vote in their interest. The same applies to the committee on pastor-parish relations where the pastor is also an ex officio member. Although, *The Book of Discipline* 2008 seems to be silent on the pastor's right to vote, statements such as, "The pastor shall be present at each meeting of the committee on pastor-parish relations . . . The committee may meet with district superintendent without the pastor . . ." (¶ 258.2), suggest that the pastor cannot vote in this committee given the fact that the committee is dealing with his or her relations with the parish.

Chapter 2

The Ministry of the Ordained

The UMC includes two types of ministry—the ministry of the ordained performed by clergy and the ministry of the laity.

> Ordination is fulfilled in leadership of the people of God through ministries of Service, Word, Sacrament, and Order. . . . Those who respond to God's call to lead in service and to equip others for this ministry through teaching, proclamation, and worship and who assist elders in the administration of the sacraments are ordained deacons. Those whose leadership in service includes preaching and teaching the Word of God, administration of the sacraments, ordering the Church for its mission and service, and administration of the *Discipline* of the Church are ordained as elders. (¶ 303.2)

An ordained minister is either deacon in full connection, or elder in full connection. This new structure launched in 1996 constitutes an important change in the UMC ministry of the ordained. The ministry of the ordained elder is by nature an itinerant ministry, while ordained deacons as well as licensed ministers do not itinerate. Licensed ministry in Africa often forms a preparatory stage or phase toward the ministry of the ordained.

Licensed for Pastoral Ministry

To be admitted to the pastoral ministry, one must first be a certified candidate and then be licensed for pastoral ministry. Candidates for licensed and ordained ministry shall inquire about the process of candidacy through their pastor, district superintendent, or another ordained minister. A person beginning candidacy for licensed or ordained ministry:

- "shall be a professing member in good standing of The United Methodist Church or a baptized participant of a recognized United Methodist campus ministry or other United Methodist ministry setting for a minimum of one (1) year;
- "shall write to the district superintendent requesting admission to the candidacy process and the assignment of a candidacy mentor. . . "
- "shall consult with the pastor" and committee on pastor or staff parish relations
- shall being recommended by the charge conference
- shall appear before the district committee on ordained ministry for examination of submitted statement of call and response to Wesley's historic questions (¶¶ 310, 311)

Candidates who complete the above requirements become certified candidates. Their progress shall be reviewed annually by the district committee on ordained ministry. The candidate enrolled in a school of theology, university or college shall present annually to the district committee on ordained ministry an official transcript from the school the person is attending as evidence of the progress.

In summary, a candidate for pastoral ministry starts at the local church level, and when approved by the charge conference, the candidate is recommended to district level for the individual to become a certified candidate who can enroll in theological training.

Becoming licensed for pastoral ministry follows becoming a certified candidate. A person licensed for pastoral ministry is any person not ordained as elder but who is "appointed to preach and conduct divine worship and perform the duties of a pastor," including:

- Provisional elders commissioned by the annual conference
- Local pastors . . .
- Deacons in full connection, seeking to qualify for ordination as an elder, [and]
- Licensed or ordained clergy from other denominations who . . . do not meet the educational requirements for provisional membership. (¶ 315)

Licensed persons for pastoral ministry approved by the district "may be licensed by the bishop to perform all the duties of a pastor, including the sacraments of baptism and Holy Communion as well as the service of marriage . . . , burial, confirmation, and membership reception . . . while appointed to a particular charge . . ." (¶ 316.1). The district committee or the board of ordained ministry shall renew licensed pastors annually. Persons licensed for pastoral ministry may serve on any board, commission, or committee with voice and vote, except on matters of clergy character, qualifications, status, and ordination. They shall not be eligible to vote on or serve as delegates to the General or central conference. Their membership is in the annual conference even though they are not itinerant.

Local Pastors (¶¶ 318–319)

A local pastor is a certified candidate who has completed prescribed studies and qualifies as licensed for pastoral ministry. A full-time local pastor devotes his or her entire time to the church in the charge to which he or she is appointed and receives cash support per annum. A full-time local pastor shall not be enrolled as a full-time student in any school. He/she shall complete the course of study curriculum within eight years, completing four courses per year.

Part-time local pastors do not devote their entire time to the charge to which they are appointed. For this reason they do not receive cash support per annum from all church sources a sum equal to or larger than the minimum base compensation established for full-time local pastors. Part-time local pastors may be appointed to small membership churches. They shall be enrolled as pre-theological or theological students and shall complete the course of study curriculum within twelve years, completing two courses per year.

A local pastor may retire following the same retirement provisions as those for clergy members.

Provisional Members (¶¶ 324–327)

Provisional members are certified candidates who have demonstrated their gifts for ministries of service and leadership, and who have met the education requirements in theological studies. They are on probation as to character, servant leadership, and effectiveness in ministry as they prepare for ordination. Past Books of Discipline call them *probationary members.*

Commissioning is the act of the church that publicly acknowledges God's call and the response, talents, gifts, and training of the candidate. Before being commissioned, provisional members shall respond to a written and oral doctrinal examination administered by the conference board of ordained ministry. Having been commissioned, provisional ministers shall be appointed by a bishop and serve a minimum of two years and a maximum of eight years following the completion of education requirements for full connection as probationary members of the annual conference. The period of commissioned ministry is concluded when the provisional members are received as full members of the annual conference and ordained as either deacon or elder, or a decision is made not to proceed toward ordination and provisional membership.

Local Ministry

The latest Africa central conference edition (1990) of *The Book of Discipline of the* UMC, uses the term *local ministry* to describe the pastoral ministry performed by unordained laypersons that do not itinerate. The local ministry includes exhorters, lay preachers, and local preachers or local pastors. Some of the terms cited above are no longer used in the UMC but they are still maintained in some annual conferences in Africa. The local ministry is useful in Africa, especially in rural areas where the church has not yet grown to have an ordained pastor in charge.

An exhorter is a voluntary worker within the local congregation constituted by the election of the charge conference in which he or she resides. An exhorter shall be required to take the course for studies for exhorters and shall be granted an annual license signed by the district superintendent. The duties of an exhorter are to hold meetings for prayers and exhortations to assist in pastoral visitation and to promote religious education.

A lay preacher is a person who has been authorized to preach regularly under the direction of the pastor or district superintendent. A lay preacher shall be constituted by the district conference or the charge conference. The person is required to complete studies for a lay preacher's license. A lay preacher has the duty to act as assistant to the pastor and may be appointed by the bishop to fill a pastoral position.

A local preacher can be compared to a local pastor. This is an unordained lay preacher who is given a pastoral charge by arrangement of the annual conference with the DS and the bishop's cabinet. The local ministry in the current UMC structure is to be compared to the stage of certified candidacy and licensed for pastoral ministry. The local ministry is a preparatory stage of the ministry of the ordained.

The Ordained Ministry

The ordained ministry of the United Methodist Church consists of deacons and elders.

> From among the baptized, deacons are called by God to a lifetime of servant leadership, authorized by the Church, and ordained by a bishop. Deacons fulfill servant ministry in the world and lead the Church in relating the gathered life of Christians to their ministries in the world, interrelating worship in the gathered community with service to God in the world. Deacons give leadership in the Church's life: in teaching and proclaiming the Word; in contributing to worship, and in assisting the elders in the administering the sacraments of baptism and the Lord's Supper; in forming and nurturing disciples; in conducting marriages and burying the dead; in embodying the church's mission to the world; and in leading congregations in interpreting the needs, concerns, and hopes of the world. . . . From the earliest days of the church, deacons were called and set apart for the ministry of love, justice, and service; of connecting the church with the most needy, neglected, and marginalized among the children of God. (¶ 328)

A candidate for ordination as deacon is required to have been a provisional member for at least two full annual conference years, having served under episcopal appointment in a ministry of service the entire commissioned period and having responded to a written or oral doctrinal examination administered by the board of ordained ministry.

Deacons are members of annual conference. Their appointments are made by the bishop but they do not itinerate. They shall have the rights of voice and vote in the annual conference where their membership is held. They shall be eligible to serve as clergy on boards, commissions, or committees of the annual conference. They shall be eligible for election as a clergy delegate to the general and central conferences. They shall share with elders responsibility for all matters of ordination, character, and conference relations of clergy. They may be appointed to salaried or non-salaried positions.

> Elders are ordained to a lifetime ministry of Word, Sacrament, Order, and Service. By the authority given in their ordination they are authorized to preach and teach the Word of God, to provide pastoral care and counsel, to administer the sacraments of baptism and Holy Communion, and to order the life of the Church for service in mission and ministry. The servant leadership of the elder, in both parish and extension ministries, is expressed by leading the people of God in worship and prayer, by leading persons to faith in Jesus Christ, by exercising pastoral supervision, and by ordering the Church in mission in the world. (¶ 332)

A candidate for ordination as elder is required to have been a provisional member for at least two years, served full-time under episcopal appointment for at least two full annual conference years, and met the educational requirements. He or she shall prepare and preach at least one written sermon on a biblical passage specified by the board of ordained ministry and shall respond to a written or oral doctrinal examination administered by the board of ordained ministry.

Elders are members of the annual conference, ordained and appointed by a bishop. They itinerate and offer themselves without reserve to be appointed and to serve, after consultation as the appointive authority may determine. They annually participate in a process of evaluation with committee on pastor-parish relations and with the district superintendent. Elders in full connection share with deacons in full connection responsibility for matters of ordination, character, and conference relations of clergy. They shall be eligible to be elected delegates to the general and central conferences.

The Diaconal Ministry and the Ordained Ministry

The Books of Discipline of the UMC from 1992 onwards use the term *diaconal ministry* that is no longer in use in the UMC since 1996. The diaconal ministry referred to the ministry of laypersons set apart for service in the church and the world. Those people were previously called lay deacons, or diaconal ministers. They participated with the elders in the leadership of worship in the church and were used as assistant pastors though they were laypersons. They were consecrated diaconal ministers by a bishop at the annual conference session. Diaconal ministers served in non-itinerant ministries. They were eligible for election as lay delegates to the general or central conference.

The history of African Methodism reveals that headmasters, teachers, and nurses in church institutions were consecrated as diaconal ministers to support the few ordained ministers in the local church. Their matters were dealt with by the board of diaconal ministry.

The ordained ministry included another category of deacons called ordained deacons. They constituted the order of deacons and they were part of the clergy. They were ordained by a bishop and were in preparation to become elders in full connection after at least two years in ministry as deacons.

The 1996 General Conference made an important change regarding the orders of ministry. The diaconal ministry was incorporated into the ministry of the ordained deacon.

There are no longer lay deacons, or diaconal ministers, in the church, except those who have been consecrated as such before the 1996 General Conference.

The current order of deacons is independent from the order of elders. The ministry of the deacon is no longer a transitional stage leading to the ministry of the elder. A deacon, like an elder, is a member in full connection for life, although a deacon can apply to become elder and vice versa.

The church in Africa has not yet managed to implement these changes. Throughout the church in Africa one still finds lay deacons and provisional members ordained as itinerant deacons preparing for ordination as elders. Ordained deacons in full connection, as a new order, are scarcely found. Education requirements for one to qualify for the ministry of the ordained are not followed as stipulated in *The Book of Discipline*. Educational requirements for deacons seem to be left to the discretion of each annual conference.

Chapter 3

The Superintendency

The superintendency in the UMC is similar all over the United Methodist world. This is the chapter in UMC polity that has conserved its uniformity. This may be due to the fact that the council of bishops meets regularly and bishops strive to maintain the standards. If it happens that some acts or administration of the superintendency are unconstitutional, it may be assumed that it is done deliberately, taking advantage of the ignorance of church members and ministers. The superintendency resides in the office of bishop and extends to the district superintendent, with each possessing district and collegial responsibilities. It constitutes a special ministry, not a separate order (¶¶ 401 and 402).

Bishops

Bishops are elders in full connection who are elected from the order of elders and they are:

> set apart for a ministry of servant leadership, general oversight and supervision (¶ 401). As followers of Jesus Christ, bishops are authorized to guard the faith, order, liturgy, doctrine, and discipline of the Church. The role and calling forth of the bishop is to exercise oversight and support of the Church in its mission of making disciples of Jesus Christ for the transformation of the world. The basis of such discipleship of leadership (*episkopé*) lies in discipline and a disciplined life. (¶ 403.1)

They are elected by their respective central conferences and assigned to their respective residences in the central conferences after they are consulted by the central conference committee on episcopacy. In the United States, bishops itinerate within the five jurisdictional conferences of the country; this has not yet happened in Africa. Bishops are appointed to the annual conferences where they were members before their election as bishops.

Bishops in Africa are elected for a period of four years. If re-elected, they are elected for life (Africa Central Conference 1976). If not re-elected, he or she shall return to a full membership as an elder of the annual conference from which that person ceased to be a member when elected for the episcopacy (Africa Central Conference 1976).

Bishops are elected general superintendents of the whole church. The power to elect bishops for central conferences was referred to the central conferences in 1929. Through their election, bishops first become members of the council of bishops before they are subsequently assigned to areas of service. Central conferences and annual conferences are the areas of service to which they are assigned but are not members. At the central conference level, they are members of the college of bishops, which is a substructure of the council of bishops.

District Superintendents

District superintendents are elders in full connection appointed by the bishop to the cabinet and assigned to responsibilities of oversight and supervision within a district and in the entire annual conference. Before selecting and appointing a DS, the bishop shall consult with the cabinet and the committee on district superintendency for new assignments.

> The DS shall oversee the total ministry of the clergy and of the churches in the communities of the district in their missions of witness and service in the world: (*a*) by giving

priority to the scheduling of time and effort for spiritual leadership, pastoral support, supervision, and encouragement to the clergy and to the churches of the district; (*b*) by encouraging their personal, spiritual, and professional growth; (*c*) by encouraging their personal commitment to the mandate of inclusiveness in the life of the church; (*d*) by promoting, supporting, and modeling generous Christian giving, with special attention to teaching the biblical principles of giving; (*e*) by nominating persons to serve as guides for the ministry inquiring process; (*f*) by nominating clergy in compliance with ¶ 329.1.a,b in *The United Methodist Book of Discipline* 2004 to serve in the ministry of mentoring candidates, commissioned ministers, local pastors and other provisional members; (*g*) by participating with the bishops in the appointment-making process; (*h*) by assigning persons such as certified lay ministers to churches who do not have appointed clergy; (*i*) by enabling programs throughout the district that may assist local churches to build and extend their ministry and mission with their people and to the community; (*j*) by working in cooperation with appropriate district and annual conference agencies to explore long-range, experimental, ecumenical, multicultural, multiracial, and cooperative ministries; (*k*) to provide representation and leadership in the district in the quest for Christian unity in ministry and mission, encouraging local congregations in development of an understanding and relationship with other living faith communities and in working with ecumenical agencies and coalitions in the sharing of resources, and, where appropriate, serving as an ecumenical liaison with other living faith communities; (*l*) by assisting the bishop in the administration of the annual conference. (¶ 419)

The normal term for a DS shall be up to six years, but this may be extended to no more than eight years at the discretion of the bishop, in consultation with the cabinet and the district committee on superintendency. District superintendents are members of the cabinet before they are subsequently assigned by the bishop to service in districts. The cabinet is the annual conference body composed of the bishop and the district superintendents.

Appointment-making

Appointment-making in Africa is often a crucial and stressful time during an annual conference session mainly because of some abuses and lack of respect for the procedures that guide the process.

The appointment of clergy is made by the bishop, in consultation with and with the assistance of the cabinet. Appointments take into consideration the unique needs of a charge, the community context, and also the gifts and evidence of God's grace in a particular pastor. This means that before appointment-making, the pastor to be appointed and the congregation (through the pastor-parish relations committee) receiving the appointee, must be consulted by the district superintendent and/or the bishop. In fact, a change in appointment may be initiated by the pastor, the committee on pastor-parish relations, the district superintendent, or the bishop. The bishop and the cabinet shall consider all requests for change of appointment in light of the profile developed for each charge and the gifts and evidence of God's grace, professional experience, and family needs of the pastor.

During the process of making a new appointment, the district superintendent shall confer with the pastor about a specific possible appointment, then with the receiving committee on pastor-parish relations. If during the consultative process, it is determined by the bishop and cabinet that this decision should not be carried out, the process is to be repeated until the consultation gives a green light to the bishop to make the appointment. When the steps in the process have been followed and completed, the announcement of that decision shall be made to all parties directly involved in the consultative process—the cabinet, the pastor, and the committee on pastor-parish relations—before a public announcement is made.

If the appointment-making process follows the criteria and respects the procedure of consultation, unnecessary trouble, protests, and resignations can be avoided. The UMC works under the itinerant system. All pastors are aware of this system and offer themselves to itinerancy and the appointment-making process. What is needed is to abide by the principles of the UMC as far as appointment-making is concerned.

Chapter 4

The Conferences

The United Methodist Church is a connectional structure maintained through its chain of conferences. The church is run and organized through these conferences in which United Methodist members meet, evaluate their activities, and make plans to achieve the mission of the church in the world. The church is organized into General Conference, jurisdictional and central conferences, annual conferences, and district conferences. Because the General Conference includes the entire church and impacts all conferences, the UMC polity is the same across the world. Some differences are evident in African United Methodist conferences for two reasons: 1) There is a disciplinary provision for central conferences to adapt *The Book of Discipline* in light of context, but also 2) there is lack of an edited and up-to-date *Book of Discipline* for the central conferences. This chapter will highlight major changes that have occurred over recent years in order to update the African UMC polity.

General Conference

The General Conference is the United Methodist general gathering, every four years, of annual and central conference delegates from the entire world. The General Conference is the legislative body of the church. No person, no paper, and no organization has the authority to speak officially for the UMC; this right is reserved exclusively for the General Conference. At General Conference new laws and changes are introduced and proposed through petitions from any organization, clergy member, or lay member of the UMC. Few petitions come from

African delegates. Africans have complained about the passage of some regulations that are not fitting for the African context.

Delegates at the General Conference shall be elected by annual conferences, not appointed. Lay delegates shall be elected by lay members without regard to age. This gives room for youth participation at General Conference and nullifies the 1944 *Discipline of the Methodist Church in Africa* that determines the minimum age of twenty-five for delegates.

Central Conferences

Central conferences are regional conferences. Africa has three central conferences: the Africa Central Conference, the Congo Central conference, and the West Africa Central Conference.

> A central conference shall have power to make such changes and adaptations of the *Book of Discipline* as the special conditions and mission of the church in the area require, especially concerning the organization and administration of the work on local church, district, and annual conference levels, provided that no action shall be taken that is contrary to the Constitution and the General Rules of the United Methodist Church, and provided that the spirit of connectional relationship is kept between the local and the general church. (¶ 543.7)
>
> A central conference shall have authority to edit and publish a central conference *Discipline*, which shall contain in addition to the Constitution of the Church such sections from the general *Discipline* of The United Methodist Church . . . and also such revised, adapted, or new sections as shall have been enacted by the central conference concerned under the powers given by the General Conference. (¶ 543.16)

Concerning the above powers of the central conference, Africa is far behind in applying them. Since 1990, no change, no adaptation, and no new sections have been brought to the central conference edition of *The Book of Discipline*, especially in the Congo Central Conference and the Africa Central Conference. Accordingly, the UMC polity is diverse and the United Methodist connectionalism is being lost.

The Annual Conference

> The purpose of the annual conference is to make disciples of Jesus Christ for the transformation of the world by equipping its local churches for ministry and by providing a connection for ministry beyond the local church; all to the glory of God. (¶ 601)

The annual conference is the basic body of the UMC. Like the General Conference and central conference, it is composed of clergy and lay members. The clergy membership shall consist of deacons and elders in full connection, provisional members, associate members, affiliate members, and local pastors under appointment to a pastoral charge.

> The lay membership of the annual conference shall consist of a professing member elected by each charge, diaconal ministers [consecrated before 1996], deaconesses, home missioners, the conference president of United Methodist Women, the conference president of United Methodist Men, the conference lay leader, district lay leaders, the conference scouting coordinator, the president or equivalent officer of the conference young adult organization, the president of the conference youth organization, one youth between the ages of twelve and eighteen and one young person between the ages of eighteen and thirty from each

> district . . . and the chair of the annual conference college student organization. If the lay membership should number less than the clergy members of the annual conference, the annual conference shall, by its own formula, provide for the election of additional lay members to equalize lay and clergy membership of the annual conference. (¶ 602.4)

The lay members mentioned above are effective members of annual conferences. They are not to be considered as observers. Charge conferences and district conferences should sit together and make sure the effective lay members of annual conferences residing in their local churches are assigned a clergy member to meet the equal number membership of the annual conference. Special attention should be given to youth representatives to annual conferences. Youth are sometimes neglected and not considered when it comes to annual conference delegation. The same applies to the chair of an annual conference college student organization. One wonders if such a position exists in Africa since the church in Africa does possess colleges and United Methodist-related institutions.

The bishop assigned to an annual conference shall preside over the annual conference. In the absence of the bishop, the conference shall by ballot elect a president pro tempore from among the traveling elders. The president thus elected shall discharge all duties of a bishop except ordination.

Lay members cannot vote on matters of ordination, character, and conference relations of clergy. However, since the 1996 amendment, the board of ordained ministry shall have laypeople as effective members. Each annual conference shall elect at least one-fifth laypersons, and may at its discretion elect more lay members, up to one-third of the membership of the board of ordained ministry. Therefore, lay members of the conference board of ordained ministry may vote on matters of ordination, character, and conference relations of clergy. The amendment has superseded ¶ 448.2 of *The Book of Discipline of the* UMC *Africa Central Conference Edition* stating, "Lay members shall serve on all committees except those on ordained ministerial relations and for trial of clergy." Unfortunately, up to now this amendment is rarely implemented in Africa.

The board of ordained ministry shall select from its own membership an official representative to serve as member of each district committee on ordained ministry.

There shall be a conference committee on episcopacy composed at least of seven but no more than seventeen, elected by the annual conference. The committee shall consist of one-third laywomen, one-third laymen, and one-third clergypersons. It works with the bishop the way the pastor-parish relations committee does with the pastor in charge at the local church level.

It is recommended that each annual conference have a director of connectional ministries to focus and guide the mission and ministry of the UMC within the annual conference. The director may be lay or clergy. The director shall serve as an officer of the annual conference and shall sit with the cabinet when the cabinet considers matters relating to coordination, implementation, or administration of the conference program. This recommendation is not yet implemented in many annual conferences in Africa. Each annual conference, on nomination of its council on finance and administration, shall elect a conference treasurer or conference treasurer/director of administrative services. The elected treasurer shall be directly amenable to the council.

"After consultation with the bishop in charge, the council may remove the . . . treasurer/director from office for cause and fill the vacancy until the next session of the conference" (¶ 619). One would wonder why by and large treasurers are appointed and amenable to bishops instead of being elected by annual conferences, and amenable to the council on finance and administration.

Conference Agencies

> The annual conference is responsible for structuring its ministries and administrative procedures in order to accomplish its purpose . . . In so doing it shall provide for the connectional relationship of the local church, district, and conference with the general agencies. . . .
>
> 1. An annual conference shall provide for the functions and General Conference connections with all general agencies provided by the *Discipline* as follows: *a*) There shall be clear connections between the General Conference agencies, annual conference program and administrative entities, and the local congregation; *b*) There shall be clear checks and balances regarding program functions and financial/administration functions within the annual conference. In doing this, the annual conference may organize units so long as the functions of ministry are fulfilled and the connectional relationships are maintained.
> 2. The annual conference may appoint additional committees for the purpose of promoting the work of The United Methodist Church within the bounds of the said annual conference and may prescribe their membership and their powers and duties. (¶ 610)

Conference agencies include:

- conference council on finance and administration
- commission on equitable compensation
- board of church and society
- board of discipleship
- conference board of laity
- Committee on Ethnic Local Church Concerns

- board of global ministries
- committee on parish and community development
- board of higher education and campus ministry
- Board of Ordained Ministry
- administrative review committee
- conference committee on episcopacy
- conference board of pensions
- board of trustees
- conference commission on archives and history
- conference commission or committee on Christian unity and interreligious concerns
- conference commission on religion and race
- conference commission on the status and role of women
- conference commission on the small membership church
- commission on communications
- United Methodist Women
- United Methodist Men
- conference council on youth ministry
- conference council on young-adult ministry
- conference council on older-adult ministries
- committee on Native American ministry
- conference Advance program
- committee on criminal justice and mercy ministries

Agencies are organized in a way that corresponds to the general agencies of the UMC and they are put into place so that there may be connections from the local church to the general church. The annual conference may appoint additional committees for the purpose of promoting the work of the UMC within the bounds of the said annual conference and may prescribe their membership and their powers and duties. Some of the committees and commissions have been put into in place to meet American and western United Methodist problems.

Africans can replace them with those that have to do with the African UMC concerns, like commissions on tribalism, ministry to minority groups, and culture and worship.

Other committees and commissions are not yet understood in some areas. Accordingly, when people meet and discuss matters pertaining to the respective committees, resolutions that are taken are not consistent, and no one is expecting receiving anything out of it because of ignorance. Many annual conferences, districts, and local churches have missed some opportunities to grow with the assistance of committees and commissions ignoring their rights and privileges.

The District Conference

A district conference may be organized in an annual conference. Its membership generally includes more lay members than clergy members. At the district level, the principle of equal number of clergy and laity does not apply. A district conference shall be held upon the call of the district superintendent.

There shall be the district committee on ordained ministry that is amenable to the annual conference through the Board of Ordained Ministry. This committee shall be composed of a representative from the Board of Ordained Ministry, the district superintendent, at least six other clergy in the district, and at least three professing members of local churches who will be full participating members with votes.

There shall be a committee on district superintendency, which shall be composed of eleven members including the district lay leaders and two persons appointed by the district superintendent. At least three of the eleven persons shall be clergy persons and seven shall be laypersons (men, women, and young people). The committee will work with the district superintendent, playing the role of pastor-parish relations committee in the local church.

Chapter 5

Agencies

Agencies in the UMC are important tools in the accomplishment of God's mission. They are an expression of connectionalism dealing with global church matters from the General Conference to the local church. In *The Book of Discipline of the United Methodist Church*, agencies, under the title *administrative order* occupy almost one-third of the *Discipline*, demonstrating their importance. Unfortunately, the church in Africa is not well informed about these agencies. The central conference books of discipline do not emphasize or describe them. Connections between the local church, the annual conference, the central conference, and the general conference are poor. This deprives Africa of benefitting from the full input of these agencies and their programs.

General Provisions

> General agencies, in particular, are important to our common vision, mission, and ministry. They provide essential services and ministries beyond the scope of individual local congregations and annual conferences through services and ministries that are highly focused, flexible, and capable of rapid response. The general agencies of The United Methodist Church are the regularly established councils, boards, commissions, committees, or other units with ongoing responsibilities that have been constituted by the General Conference. (¶ 701.3)

Agencies operating at the general church level are called general agencies.

Two general agencies provide oversight, accountability, and coordination of other agencies on behalf of the General Conference. They are called councils. These are:

- The General Council on Finance and Administration (GCFA) and
- The Connectional Table (CT) previously called General Council on Ministries (GCOM)

Four other general agencies are called boards. They inform and implement the vision and programs of the General Conference. These are as follows:

- General Board of Church and Society (GBCS)
- General Board of Global Ministries (GBGM)
- General Board of Discipleship (GBOD) and
- General Board of Higher Education and Ministry (GBHEM)

Other general agencies fulfill special functions. They are administrative and support units:

- General Board of Pension and Health Benefits (GBPHB)
- General Commission on Archives and History (GCAH)
- General Commission on Communication (GCOC) and
- United Methodist Publishing House (UMPH)

The last group comprises advocacy commissions:

- General Commission on the Status and Role of Women (GCSRW)
- General Commission on United Methodist Men (GCUMM)
- General Commission on Christian Unity and Interreligious Concerns (GCCUIC) and
- General Commission on Religion and Race (GCRR)

Between sessions of General Conference, general boards and general commissions are accountable to the Connectional Table. All general agencies receiving general church funds shall account for receipts and expenditures of funds in a format designed by the General Council on Finance and Administration.

The general agency membership includes members elected from jurisdictional conferences, nominated by central conference, and bishops nominated by the council of bishops.

General Duties of Agencies

"The purpose of the Connectional Table (CT) is for the discernment and articulation of the vision for the church and the stewardship of the mission, ministries, and resources of The United Methodist Church as determined by the actions of the General Conference and in consultation with the Council of Bishops" (¶ 904).

The General Council on Finance and Administration coordinates and administers The United Methodist Church's finances in accord with general conference legislative actions; receives, disburses, and accounts for the church's general funds (Section II. ¶¶ 801–823).

The General Board of Church and Society implements Social Principles and other policy statements of the General Conference on Christian social concerns (Section IV, ¶¶ 1001–1011).

The primary purpose of the General Board of Discipleship

> shall be to assist annual conferences, districts, and local churches of all membership sizes in their efforts to win persons to Jesus Christ as his disciples and to help these persons to grow in their understanding of God that they may respond in faith and love, to the end that they may know who they are and what their human situation means, increasingly identifying themselves as children of God

> and members of the Christian community, to live in the Spirit of God in every relationship, to fulfill their common discipleship in the world, and to abide in the Christian hope. (¶ 1101.1)

The work of the GBOD focuses primarily on the local church, helping congregations to win converts to the Christian faith; nurtures spiritual life and increased personal commitment; oversees Christian education; provides resources in Christian education, evangelism, lay ministries, spiritual growth, stewardship, worship, and training in devotional life and leadership; administers United Methodist youth ministry; and enriches local church discipleship ministries. The Division on Ministries with Young People falls under this agency.

The General Board of Global Ministries seeks "to discern those places where the gospel has not been heard or heeded and to witness to its meaning throughout the world, inviting all persons to newness of life in Jesus Christ through a program of global ministries" (¶ 1302). The GBGM enables congregations and annual conferences to participate in mission activity; challenges United Methodists to proclaim the Christian faith around the world; recruits, sends, and receives missionaries across racial, cultural, national, and political boundaries; promotes Christian unity through witness and service with ecumenical councils and churches; and supports women in their mission commitment and leadership. The Women's Division and the United Methodist Committee on Relief (UMCOR) are under this general board.

The General Board of Higher Education and Ministry "exists . . . for the specific purpose of preparing and assisting persons to fulfill their ministry in Christ in the several special ministries, ordained and diaconal; and to provide general oversight and care for campus ministries and institutions of higher education, including schools, colleges, universities, and theological schools" (¶ 1404). The board prepares persons for ordained and designated ministries in United Methodism around the world; maintains relationships with individuals in these ministries; and represents the church in higher education. The Division of Higher Education and the Division of Ordained Ministry are found under this agency.

The General Board of Pension and Health Benefits exists "to operate, manage, and administer the mandatory benefit funds, plans, and programs established by the General Conference" (¶ 1504.1). The board serves United Methodist clergy, lay employees, and other church workers and their families through retirement and other benefit programs. It seeks with the assistance of other boards and agencies to establish a pension system for central conference pastors.

The General Commission on Archives and History cares for the historical interests of the UMC. The commission gathers, preserves and disseminates archival materials. (Section XI, ¶¶ 1701–1712)

The General Commission on Communication, commonly known by the name United Methodist Communications, "shall meet the communication, public relations, and marketing needs of the entire Church, reflecting the cultural and racial diversity within The United Methodist Church" (¶1805). The commission provides communications programs and services that enable more effective Christ-centered ministry across the connected congregations; promote denominational funds and programs; gather and distribute church news; produce broadcast and cable television programs; and provide communications resources to local churches and annual conferences.

The General Commission on Christian Unity and Interreligious Concerns exists "to advocate and work toward the full reception of the gift of Christian unity" and "to advocate and work for the establishment and strengthening of relationships with other living faith communities" (¶ 1902). The commission seeks to help United Methodists realize the church's ecumenical commitment and to understand their membership in the one church of Jesus Christ; seeks to discern and advocate God's plan for the unity of the human community; and develops training for ecumenical leadership among United Methodists.

The General Commission on Religion and Race exists "to challenge and equip the general agencies, institutions, and connectional structures of The United Methodist Church to a full and equal participation of the racial and ethnic constituency in the total life and mission of the Church" (¶ 2002). The commission assists annual conferences in developing programs and policies designed to achieve inclusiveness.

The General Commission on the Status and Role of Women exists "to challenge The United Methodist Church, including its general agencies, institutions, and connectional structures, to a continuing commitment to the full and equal responsibility and participation of women in the total life and mission of the Church, sharing fully in the power and in the policy-making at all levels of the Church's life" (¶ 2102).

The commission advocates for women within the church; develops policies and strategies to address and eradicate all forms of sexism; and develops guidelines for language that is inclusive of all persons and reflective of the fullness of God.

The General Commission on United Methodist Men "shall have primary oversight for the coordination and resourcing of men's ministry within The United Methodist Church" (¶ 2302). The commission coordinates resources on evangelism, mission, stewardship, spiritual development, and men's role in society; and prepares United Methodist Men leaders.

The objectives of the United Methodist Publishing House shall be:

> the advancement of the cause of Christianity throughout the world by disseminating religious knowledge and useful literacy, scientific, and educational information in the form of books, tracts, multimedia, electronic media, and periodicals; the promotion of Christian education; the implementation of any and all activities properly connected

> with the publishing, manufacturing in a variety of media, and distribution of books, tracts, periodicals, materials, and supplies for churches and church schools . . . (¶ 1613)

The Publishing House supports and extends Christian formation by providing resource materials and related services through the ministries of individuals, congregations, and the connectional church; disseminates education, inspiration, scholarly, and practical books, curriculum resources, periodicals, electronic products, church supplies, sanctuary and school equipment, choir robes, and other products.

Chapter 6

Governance

The United Methodist Church is governed by three bodies: the General Conference, the Council of Bishops, and the Judicial Council. The General Conference is the legislative body of the UMC. It has already been described in Chapter 3.

The Council of Bishops

> Bishops, although elected by jurisdictional or central conferences, are elected general superintendents of the whole Church. . . . By virtue of their election and consecration, bishops are members of the Council of Bishops and are bound in special covenant with all other bishops. In keeping with this covenant, bishops fulfill their servant leadership and express their mutual accountability. The Council of Bishops is a faith community of mutual trust and concern responsible for the faith development and continuing well-being of its members. (¶ 427)

The council provides spiritual leadership for the church, helping to set the direction of the church and its mission throughout the world. Historically, bishops preside over the General Conference, central conferences, and annual conferences.

The Judicial Council

The Judicial Council is the highest judicial body, or court, in The United Methodist Church (¶¶ 55–57 of The Constitution and ¶¶ 2609–2612).

The Council determines the constitutionality of acts, or proposed acts, of the general, jurisdictional, annual, or central conferences, either on appeal or through request for declaratory decisions; determines whether acts of official bodies of the church conform to *The Book of Discipline*; and reviews decisions of law made by presiding bishops. Its membership, comprised of both clergy and laypeople, is elected by the General Conference.

Conclusion and Recommendations

The United Methodist Church is a well-organized church. Its polity changes nearly every four years in order to adapt to the changing realities of the world. In the two decades since 1990, when the last Africa Central Conference edition of *The Book of Discipline* was published, a series of important adaptations, innovations, and changes have been brought to UMC polity.

Empowering the Laity

The emergence of the church council at the local church level remains an important innovation in local church leadership involving large numbers of laypeople in the ministry of all believers. The laity has been given full responsibility in church business. They chair committees and commissions and are involved in church decision making. The church is moving towards the full empowerment of laity, removing completely the legacy of an earlier Methodism that often relegated laypeople to secondary rank in church leadership and that led to the creation of the Methodist Protestant Church as a sign of lay protestation. Being empowered, laity become partners in ministry with clergy and cease to consider themselves victims of clergy. The promise of lay empowerment is holistic church growth and the reduction of unnecessary tensions between laity and clergy as far as church leadership is concerned.

By making district and even local church lay leaders members of the annual conference, *The Book of Discipline* shows that the church is to prepare lay leaders to play their role effectively in the church. This practical provision for lay empowerment in the church facilitates the transmission of original and updated church resolutions from laity to laity, thus avoiding lapses and selective transmission of resolutions. This particularly helps to preserve and pass on a correct understanding of the purpose and mission of the church against the wrong images that some leaders communicate. The mission of the church remains that of making disciples of all people as described in the gospel according to Matthew 28:19–20.

One of the most important innovations in UMC polity is the incorporation of laypeople as members of the board of ordained ministry with voice and vote. This shows how the church is giving credit to laity as partners in ministry with clergy; it helps to demystify the ministry of the ordained, long considered as unaccountable to laity.

As of now, few annual conferences are implementing this resolution to include laity on the board of ordained ministry because there are those who want to maintain the board of ordained ministry as off limits to laity. The UMC, however, believes in the ministry of all believers. There is no minister in the church who was not a layperson before becoming clergy. The board of ordained ministry is like other boards, the only difference being that it is dealing with matters pertaining to ministers and those who want to become ministers. There is nothing wrong with laity participating on this board and contributing to the betterment of the pastoral ministry. Laypeople who share pastors' concerns can become good advocates of pastors in the church; they can remove the impression that the board functions to cover up pastors' misdoings and blunders.

Raising Up the Young People

The incorporation of youth as delegates of the general conference and effective members of the annual conferences is a change that the church has made to honor and prepare the younger generation for church leadership. There was a time when youth were considered useless in the church. They were said to be the church for tomorrow. But this is missing the point. Youth are efficient workers in the church. They are potential leaders, capable of learning and understanding church matters and making positive contributions. They follow the example of Jesus Christ who was able to deal with church business at the age of twelve ,as described in Luke 2:41–52. Churches must give youth opportunities to serve in the church no matter what it costs.

The resolution to empower youth is not yet implemented in most of our churches, in part because of a tendency in African culture that does not see anything good coming from Nazareth (John 1:46). Nowadays, youth in Africa have proved their worth in churches that have made use of them. Some churches advance financial constraints that prevent district youth delegates' attendance at annual conferences. But churches must budget for this, knowing youth cannot raise conference fees by themselves. The future of the UMC is bright if we will incorporate gifted youth in leadership positions in the church.

Providing Two Orders of Ordained Ministry

The organization of the ministry of the ordained into two orders, the order of the deacon and the order of the elder, has revolutionized the ministry of the ordained following the biblical model found in the book of Acts 6:1–6. The church in Africa still needs more elders than deacons. But in providing two orders, the church seems to have understood that the harvest is plenty but workers are few (Matt. 9:37–38). On the ground in Africa, however, we have many ministers who work more as deacons than elders. The reasons are simple. Some do not work full-time in the parishes, seeking for other means of survival outside their pastoral charge. Others are more comfortable with the roles of deacons than of elders, finding them less demanding. But because the church in Africa does not offer them the option of being ordained deacons, they remain elders against their wishes—to the detriment of the pastoral ministry in the church.

As the church grows in Africa, we need to implement the order of deacon and to consider the future ministry of the clergy. Otherwise, if we leave the full weight of leadership on the shoulders of the elders, their numbers will decrease because of hardships and lack of sufficient ministerial support. Besides, the existence of the order of deacons will help the church have qualified ministers to deal with specific ministries. So far the church in Africa lacks this category of worker, although it needs it. The existence of deacons will also help to reduce clergy dependency on church resources. Deacons are able to be self-supportive.

Consultation in the Appointment-Making Process

The provision of consultation during the appointment-making process of ordained ministers is a remarkable revelation in the church that if followed by all concerned parties can help perpetuate itinerancy. Itinerancy is a United Methodist system in which pastors are appointed by bishops, a system being threatened nowadays. The crucial moment of annual conference sessions is the appointment time. By and large, ministers are not consulted before their appointments. They are surprised with the news the day of the appointment. The process is therefore taken either as punishment or as a favor. Due to such misinterpretation, it loses its meaning. Accordingly, some of those who are discontent with their appointment end up by protesting or simply resigning.

The appointment-making process has become a problem to the superintendency as well as to ministers themselves. Conferences have few viable parishes in terms of ministerial support. By and large parishes are not able to support a pastor and his or her family. Yet all ministers wish to be appointed to a viable parish. There is the dilemma. In order to mitigate the discontentment, the consultation process can serve to clarify and explain the situation facing the church, leading to the consent of ministers. Consulting with pastors will be a therapy to the crisis that the itinerancy system is facing.

Utilizing the Agencies

Light shone on agencies in the UMC has served to open the local church to these important tools for accomplishing its mission. Agencies serve as facilitators of connectional ministries from the local church to the general church. They help with resources to achieve connectional ministries' goals. Unfortunately, in Africa little is known of agencies. One of the major reasons for this is that past editions of the Africa Central Conference Books of Discipline were mute on agencies or poorly described them. This has left the church ignorant and has contributed to diminished connectionalism through the UMC in Africa.

Recommendations

The UMC, being a connectional church, moves together at the same pace in implementing the changes over the United Methodist world. That is what is expected of the church in Africa. This leads to some recommendations:

1. Central conferences in Africa must publish regularly updated central conference editions of *The Book of Discipline*, which will inform and update the church on UMC polity. Non-English speaking annual conferences need *The Book of Discipline* translated into French and Portuguese. Twenty years without an updated Book of Discipline in a church that updates the general Book of Discipline every four years is unacceptable. How can United Methodists in Africa claim to belong to the UMC without moving together with others using the same polity? Africa has to take steps to provide for the publication of UMC polity, starting with the Book of Discipline.

   According to *The Book of Discipline* 2008:

   > In a central conference or provisional central conference using a language other than English, legislation passed by a General Conference shall not take effect until twelve months after the close of that General Conference in order to afford the necessary time to

> make adaptations and to publish a translation of the legislation that has been enacted, the translation to be approved by the resident bishop or bishops of the central conference. (¶ 543.17)

The general conference has even given time to central conferences to make adaptations and translations of some legislation passed at its session. This is to enforce the publication of resources from central conferences and also their translations in French, Portuguese, and English.

2. After the General Conference has been held, delegates to the gathering must work to inform their respective churches of changes and innovations that have occurred in church polity. This is to be done during the four years following the General Conference session. For this process to succeed, we need to consider and elect delegates to General and central conferences who are able to play this role.
3. Annual conferences have to systematically work to implement what has been decided at the General Conference. An *ad hoc* commission can be constituted that is composed of delegates who will work to have resolutions of the General and central conferences implemented during the quadrennium.
4. *The Book of Discipline of the United Methodist Church* must be accessible to all church members. In church history, before the Reformation, believers were not allowed to read the Bible by themselves. They expected priests and bishops to read and interpret it for them. But with the Reformation in the sixteenth century, Martin Luther argued that believers could read the Bible themselves and make up their own minds. This also should apply to the use of *The Book of Discipline*. It must be available for sale in bookstores and for

consultation in church offices and libraries. The same can be said of the official journals of annual conference sessions.

5. Issues of UMC polity must be regularly discussed in workshops, conferences, and other church gatherings.

The UMC is a well-structured and organized church. Its administration and organization allow its members to work and move smoothly wherever they are found. Its clergy and laity are involved in the ministry of all believers. The itinerant system and connectionalism are fully achieved in the UMC because of its organization. Its ministers work according to these systems and contribute to expand the church and to develop discipleship. Its gatherings (conferences) serve to review its policy, to adjust, and eventually adapt it to the changing conditions of this world. Agencies are organized to facilitate connectionalism. To benefit and appreciate the good of the UMC polity, the people called United Methodists need to work together, moving at the same pace, and using the same polity. The church in Africa is invited to take big steps to join the rest of the United Methodist world as far as UMC polity is concerned.

References

Books

J. E. Kirby, *The Episcopacy in American Methodism* (Nashville: Kingswood Books, 2000).

Doctrines and Discipline of the Methodist Church in Africa (Cleveland: The Central Mission Press, 1943).

Doctrines and Discipline of the Methodist Church (Nashville: The Methodist Publishing House, 1956).

The Book of Discipline of the United Methodist Church 1980 (Nashville: The United Methodist Publishing House, 1980).

The Book of Discipline of the United Methodist Church 1984 (Nashville: The United Methodist Publishing House, 1984).

The Book of Discipline of the United Methodist Church 1988 (Nashville: The United Methodist Publishing House, 1988).

The Book of Discipline of the United Methodist Church 1988, *Africa Central Conference Edition* 1990 (Nashville: The United Methodist Publishing House,1990).

The Book of Discipline of the United Methodist Church 1992 (Nashville: The United Methodist Publishing House, 1992).

The Book of Discipline of the United Methodist Church 1996 (Nashville: The United Methodist Publishing House, 1996).

The Book of Discipline of the United Methodist Church 2000 (Nashville: The United Methodist Publishing House, 2000.)

The Book of Discipline of the United Methodist Church 2004 (Nashville: The United Methodist Publishing House, 2004).

The Book of Discipline of the United Methodist Church 2008 (Nashville: The United Methodist Publishing House, 2008)

United Methodist Handbook. *The United Methodist Church—Making Disciples for the Transformation of the World* (March 2009),

Internet

Definitions of polity on the Web (28 March 2009): en.wikipedia.org/wiki/Polity

Ex *officio member* (23 February 2010), retrieved from internet 24 June 2010: http://en.wikipedia.org/wiki/Ex_officio_member

The Official Robert's Rules of Order Website (n.d), Frequently Asked Questions, retrieved from internet 24 June 2010: http://www.robertsrules.com/faq.html

CPSIA information can be obtained
at www.ICGtesting.com
Printed in the USA
LVOW04s2311061016
507746LV00007B/18/P